LOSE WEIGHT FOR GOOD

LOW CARB DIET FOR BEGINNERS

 CookNation

LOSE WEIGHT FOR GOOD: LOW CARB DIET FOR BEGINNERS
Cleanse, Detox and Shred Fat

Disclaimer

CONTENTS

Low Carb Dinners 47

Low Carb Snacks 67

Low Carb Desserts 79

Other CookNation Titles 93

INTRODUCTION

Focusing specifically on a Low Carbs our recipes have been designed to help you initiate and manage weight loss, maintain your goal weight whilst keeping you motivated and energised along the way.

What is the Low Carb Diet?

The Low Carb Diet is very much as the name suggests; a diet that is low in carbohydrates. The Low Carb Diet largely means restricting your intake of carbohydrates whilst balancing your meals with alternative carb replacements. Reduced intake of carbohydrates is linked to weight loss and is sustainable long-term providing you do not restrict your intake of other food groups too much.

The Low Carb Diet requires little preparation; you are only required to substitute common carbohydrates, such as bread and pasta, with other foods, such as vegetables and protein. There is no calorie counting, weighing amounts or measuring portions making it simple to follow and less fuss with cooking.

Typically, whilst carbohydrate consumption is significantly reduced, your intake of fats (good fats that is) should be increased for effectiveness, and so the Low Carb Diet is often also referred to as the Low Carb High Fat Diet.

What are Carbs?

Carbohydrates are essentially sugars, starch and fibres which can be found in a wide range of food groups; technically many vegetables contain carbohydrates. When we refer to carbohydrates for the purpose of a 'low carbohydrate diet', this is specifically considering 'bad' carbohydrates. Many of these 'bad' carbohydrates are manufactured by suppliers with processed sugars and additives that distress our digestive system and actually lead to weight gain. These types of carbohydrate largely make up the typical 'carbohydrate' section of most food charts today.

Here are some specific examples of carbohydrates that should be avoided as part of the Low Carb Diet: rice, pasta, potatoes, bread, beans, sugary foods (donuts, cookies), crisps, wheat, processed foods (fast food, takeaways). There is also a particular focus in the Low Carb Diet that you should avoid any produce labelled as 'low fat' or 'diet'; these types of product tend to be high in sugar (carbohydrate) and often worse for you than their regular versions. It is a common misconception that 'fat' is bad for your body and leads to weight gain; the correct fats when eaten as part of a considered diet can enhance weight loss and help to manage your goal weight.

Why eat a Low Carb Diet?

The Low Carb Diet is largely used as a tool to manage weight loss; however there are other benefits to eating less carbs. Because of the sugar often found in many typical carbohydrates today, removing these from your diet also reduces your sugar intake as well. These sugars are lead to cravings and that desire for 'something sweet' without you even realising it. When you reduce intake of these sugars your body begins to stop craving sugar within a short period of time. Therefore, you are not only likely to lose weight as a result of not eating as many carbohydrates, but you are also likely to lose weight due to reduced cravings for sugary foods.

As well as aiding weight loss a Low Carb Diet can help reduce bloating and gas as well as some of the stomachs aches and pains sometimes associated with too many 'bad' carbs.

Many people undertake the Low Carb Diet because it is so simple to manage. You know which foods to avoid and which to eat freely! This ensures that dieting doesn't take over your entire life – no calorie counting or measuring portions. Plus, it is easy to eat out as you do not need to try to guestimate the calorific content of foods and most restaurants now will happily replace carbohydrate accompaniments, such as chips, with your preferred alternatives, such as salad or vegetables.

How to eat Low Carb

As with most diets, there are various levels and extremities of a Low Carb Diet, depending on how strict you wish to be and how much weight you wish to lose. For a very strict approach, one may look to remove all carbohydrate and associated foods, such as potatoes, all grains and wheat, bread, pastas, cereal, rice, crackers, breadsticks and products labelled 'diet' and 'low fat', in addition to sugary spin offs such as sweets, sugary drinks including energy drinks, fizzy drinks and fruit.

A more relaxed approach may include small amounts of fruit, some rice and oats and some potatoes.

The Low Carb Diet can be interpreted as strictly as you wish, however, by strictly and significantly reducing your intake of carbohydrates, quicker effects will be seen, i.e. a greater weight loss. However, the flexibility with a Low Carb Diet provides that once you are happy with your weight, you may wish to become more liberal and gradually reintroduce some carbs back into your diet

How you lose weight on a Low Carb Diet

Essentially, the fewer carbohydrates you include with your diet the greater weight loss you will see!

The concept of a Low Carb Diet is actually very simple: Removing, or restricting, carbohydrates from your diet results in your body producing less insulin. This is why Low Carb Diets are often prescribed for Type 2 Diabetes sufferers. In the absence of insulin, your body begins to source its energy from fat and protein supplies, essentially burning fat. With your body using fat to fuel itself, significant weight loss effects can be experienced.

It is important to note that you may experience some initial side effects; fat cannot be used as an energy source by all parts of the body, for example the brain, and so your body produces ketones to keep everything working properly. Whilst ketones cause no harm, the release of them is referred to as ketosis and some of the side effects of this can be tiredness, headaches and bad breath. These effects can reduce over time, or you may wish to introduce a proportion of carbohydrates to help combat if you are particularly suffering.

About CookNation

CookNation is the leading publisher of innovative and practical recipe books for the modern, health conscious cook.

CookNation titles bring together delicious, easy and practical recipes with their unique no-nonsense approach - making cooking for diets and healthy eating fast, simple and fun.

With a range of #1 best-selling titles - from the innovative 'Skinny' calorie-counted series, to the 5:2 Diet Recipes collection - CookNation recipe books prove that 'Diet' can still mean 'Delicious'!

Visit **www.bellmackenzie.com** to browse the full catalogue.

 **CookNation**

low carb
breakfast
recipes

Cinnamon Almond Porridge

CLEANSE DETOX & SHRED FAT

Ingredients

- 2 tbsp almond meal
- 2 tbsp flaxseed powder
- 1 tbsp vanilla protein powder
- 1 cup/250 ml unsweetened almond milk

- ½ tsp ground cinnamon
- 2 tsp maple syrup
- Water as required

Method

1 Combine all the dry ingredients in a bowl.

2 Begin to heat almond milk in a small pan. Add the dry ingredients slowly to the milk, stirring well.

3 Continue heating and stirring for a few minutes until the porridge thickens.

4 If it is too thick, add a little water slowly.

5 Serve into a bowl and drizzle with maple syrup.

Chefs Note....
Add a spoonful of almond butter for an extra nutty fix.

Easy Breakfast Waffles

CLEANSE DETOX & SHRED FAT

Ingredients

- 60g/2½oz almond flour
- 2 medium eggs
- 120ml/½ cup milk
- 1 tbsp olive oil

- ½ tsp baking powder
- 1 tsp vanilla extract
- 1 tsp sweetener (stevia or similar)
- Cooking oil spray

Method

1 Spray your waffle maker with a little oil and heat it up.

2 Mix all the wet ingredients in a large bowl.

3 Slowly add flour and baking powder, whisking in until smooth.

4 Cook in a waffle maker according to instructions.

5 Serve immediately, or cool and store for later.

Chefs Note....
Make a large batch and store these in the freezer for a fast breakfast solution

Choc and Strawberry Smoothie Bowl

CLEANSE DETOX & SHRED FAT

Ingredients

- ½ cup/120ml almond milk
- 1 small avocado
- 1 banana, cut into small chunks and frozen
- ½ tbsp almond butter
- ½ tbsp cocoa powder

- 5-6 almonds, coarsely chopped
- 1 tsp chia seeds
- 3-4 strawberries
- ½ tsp cocoa nibs

Method

1 Add the almond milk, avocado, banana pieces, almond butter and cocoa into a high powered blender and blend until smooth.

2 If it feels too thick, add a splash of milk.

3 Pour into a bowl and top with chia seeds, sliced strawberries, nuts and cocoa nibs.

Chefs Note....
Leave out the cocoa and add cinnamon for a different twist.

Mini Coconut Pancakes

Ingredients

- 1 oz/25g coconut flour
- ¼ cup/60ml thick coconut milk
- 3 medium sized eggs
- 2½ oz/ 60g butter
- 1 tsp vanilla extract

- 1 tsp sweetener (stevia or similar)
- ½ tsp cinnamon
- ½ tsp baking powder
- Cooking oil spray
- ½ tsp salt

Method

1 Combine eggs, milk, butter and vanilla extract together.

2 Add the flour and other dry ingredients slowly, until smooth.

3 Spray cooking oil on a pan, heat and add small ladles of mixture. Cook on both sides until fluffy and brown.

Chefs Note....
Use two tbsp of mixture for each mini pancake. Top with berries and sugar free syrup.

Breakfast Muffins

CLEANSE
DETOX &
SHRED FAT

Ingredients

- 11oz/300g almond flour
- 3oz/75g butter
- ½ cup/120ml almond milk
- 4 medium eggs
- 2 tbsp mixed seeds

- 1 tsp vanilla extract
- 1 tsp cinnamon
- Pinch of baking powder
- ½ tbsp sweetener (stevia or similar)

Method

1 Preheat the oven to 175C/350F/Gas4.

2 In a large bowl beat the eggs. Add the butter and sweetener and continue to beat.

3 Mix in almond milk and vanilla extract.

4 In a separate bowl, mix flour, baking powder and cinnamon. Slowly add the egg mixture, continuing to mix until evenly blended.

5 Stir the seeds into mixture, leaving aside a few to sprinkle on top.

6 Pour mixture into muffin cases, and sprinkle the remaining seeds on top. Bake for 15-20 minutes or until golden brown and cooked through.

Chefs Note....
For a fast and filling breakfast, split a muffin and fill with nut butter.

Crunchy Breakfast Granola

CLEANSE DETOX & SHRED FAT

Ingredients

- 2oz/50g chopped almonds
- 2oz/ 50g chopped walnuts
- 2oz/50g chopped pecans
- 3oz/75g sunflower seeds
- 1oz/ 25g dried unsweetened cranberries
- 1 tbsp chia seeds
- 1 tbsp sesame seeds

- 2 tbsp flaxseed powder
- 1 tbsp ground almond meal
- 4oz/ 125g coconut butter
- 4 tbsp sugar free syrup
- 1 tsp ground cinnamon
- 1 tsp vanilla extract
- ¼ tsp sea salt

Method

1 Preheat the oven to 175C/350F/Gas4.

2 Mix all the dry ingredients in a large bowl.

3 Gently heat the coconut butter and syrup. When it's melted combine into the bowl with the dry ingredients until small clusters start to form.

4 Spread out granola mixture on a shallow baking tray, and bake for 10-15 minutes until golden brown.

5 Allow to cool and then break up into smaller pieces.

Chefs Note....
Add to a bowl of Greek yoghurt, or have it straight with unsweetened almond milk.

Smoked Salmon Omelette

CLEANSE DETOX & SHRED FAT

Ingredients

- 2 large eggs
- 2 z/50 g smoked salmon
- Salt & Pepper

- Pinch of cayenne pepper
- Cooking oil spray

Method

1 Beat eggs in a bowl and season with plenty of salt and pepper.

2 Spray a small pan with cooking oil, heat well and pour the egg mixture in.

3 Cook on a medium heat, turning once.

4 As the second side begins to set, top omelette with smoked salmon and cayenne pepper, and fold in half to finish cooking.

5 Serve immediately.

Chefs Note....
Add half an avocado for an extra filling breakfast.

Savoury Cheese Crepes

CLEANSE DETOX & SHRED FAT

Ingredients

- 3 eggs
- ½ tbsp psyllium husk powder
- ½ tbsp cream cheese
- 2oz/50g grated cheese
- Salt & Pepper
- Cooking oil spray

Method

1 Mix one egg and egg white, along with the psyllium husk and cream cheese until smoothly combined.

2 Heat a large, flat pan and spray lightly with cooking oil.

3 Add crepe mix and spread until even across the whole pan and season well.

4 Cook on a medium temperature, flipping once.

5 Crack the remaining egg onto the crepe and add grated cheese. Top with seasoning as required. Fold the crepe carefully, continuing to cook until egg is done.

Chefs Note....
Psyllium husk powder is widely available in health foods shops and is a great source of fibre.

Flourless Protein Pancakes

SERVES ??

CLEANSE DETOX & SHRED FAT

Ingredients

- 1 medium banana
- 2 large eggs
- 1 scoop flavoured protein powder
- Cooking oil spray

Method

1 Blend the banana, eggs and protein powder until smooth.

2 Spray a pan with a little cooking oil, and pour mixture in. Turn once, and cook until golden on both sides.

3 Serve immediately.

Chefs Note....
Top with a spoonful of Greek yoghurt and a handful of berries.

SERVES 1

Greek Yoghurt and Berry Parfait

CLEANSE DETOX & SHRED FAT

Ingredients

- 1 tbsp low carb granola (see recipe P17)
- 3oz/75g fresh raspberries

- 5oz/150g Greek yoghurt
- ½ tsp sweetener (stevia or similar)

Method

1 Leave aside a few raspberries. Puree the rest with the sweetener, adding a little water if needed, until it reaches a thick syrupy consistency.

2 Add Greek yoghurt to a bowl. Layer with raspberry puree, granola and the remaining fresh raspberries.

Chefs Note....
Top with a fresh sprig of mint.

Low Carb Mug Muffin

CLEANSE DETOX & SHRED FAT

Ingredients

- 1 tbsp almond flour
- 1 scoop vanilla protein powder
- 2 tsp sweetener (stevia or similar)
- 1½ tsp baking powder

- 1 large egg
- ¼ cup/60ml almond milk
- ½ tsp vanilla extract
- 1oz/25g blueberries

Method

1 Mix the dry ingredients together.

2 Mix together the egg and milk and add to powdered ingredients.

3 Pour into a mug and cook in microwave for 60 seconds, or until just risen.

4 Cool and serve immediately.

Chefs Note....
Add chocolate chips for an indulgent breakfast treat.

Low Carb Breakfast Bars

CLEANSE DETOX & SHRED FAT

Ingredients

- 2 0z/50g almonds
- 2oz/50g walnuts
- 2oz/50g coconut flakes
- 1 tbsp almond meal

- 1½ tbsp flaxseed
- ½ tbsp black strap molasses
- 1 egg white
- 1 tsp all spice

Method

1 Preheat oven to 165C/325F/Gas3.

2 Combine all the ingredients in a food processor until blended.

3 Pour the mixture out onto a baking tray.

4 Bake for 20-25 minutes, and cut into slices while warm.

5 Leave to cool.

Chefs Note....
Make a big batch of these for a fast breakfast or snack.

Cinnamon Sticky Buns

CLEANSE DETOX & SHRED FAT

Ingredients

For dough:
- 4oz/125g almond flour
- 1 large egg
- 3½oz/ 100g grated Mozzarella cheese
- 1 tsp vanilla extract
- 1½tsp baking powder
- ¼ tsp xanthan gum

For glaze:
- 2oz/50g sweetener (stevia or similar)
- 2 tsp cinnamon
- 3½ oz/ 100g butter

Method

1 Preheat the oven to 180 C/350F/Gas4.

2 Place a large glass bowl over a pan of water. Add mozzarella into the bowl and slowly melt.

3 Gradually add all the dough ingredients stirring continuously until the mixture thickens and comes together as a dough.

4 Roll the dough out on to a baking sheet, and spread out.

5 Melt the butter and add sweetener and cinnamon, mixing in a small bowl.

6 Spread cinnamon glace over the pastry dough. Roll up the dough into a large roll, and cut into small, even pieces.

7 Place on a baking tray and bake for 15-20 minutes until risen and golden.

Chefs Note....
Top with an optional cream cheese frosting for an indulgent treat.

low carb
lunch
recipes

Spicy Chicken Burrito Bowl

Ingredients

- 1 grilled skinless chicken breast, cut into pieces
- 1 small ripe avocado, cut in small chunks
- 125g/4oz cooked quinoa grains
- Handful fresh shredded lettuce
- 5-6 cherry tomatoes, sliced
- 50g/2oz grated Cheddar cheese
- 1 clove garlic, crushed
- Splash of Worcestershire sauce
- ½ tsp dried chilli flakes
- ½ lemon, juiced
- Seasoning to taste

Method

1 Combine the garlic, Worcestershire sauce, chilli flakes, lemon juice and seasoning to make a dressing.

2 In a separate bowl combine all the other ingredients together.

3 Pour the dressing over, toss lightly, and serve immediately.

Chefs Note....
If you are not eating straight away keep the dressing stored separately to prevent the salad getting soggy.

Smoked Salmon Noodle Salad

SERVES 1

CLEANSE DETOX & SHRED FAT

Ingredients

- 50g/2oz smoked salmon
- 75g/3oz shirataki noodles, cooked according to instructions
- 50g/2oz mange tout
- 1 carrot, peeled& cut into Julienne strips
- ½ tbsp light soy sauce
- ¼ tbsp Worcestershire sauce
- ¼ tbsp sesame seed oil
- 1 clove garlic, crushed
- 1 tsp brown sugar

Method

1 Mix together the soy sauce, Worcestershire sauce, sesame oil, garlic and sugar to make a dressing.

2 Cook and drain the noodles after cooking according to instructions.

3 Combine the noodles with the prepared vegetables and smoked salmon pieces.

4 Pour the dressing over and toss lightly before serving.

Chefs Note....
Shirataki noodles (also known as miracle noodles) are very low in carbs and calories.

Chilli Lettuce Tacos

CLEANSE DETOX & SHRED FAT

Ingredients

- 8oz/225g lean beef mince
- 1 small onion, diced
- ½ tsp ground cumin
- 1 tsp chilli flakes
- 2 cloves garlic, crushed

- 7oz/200g tinned sweetcorn, drained
- ½ head Romaine lettuce
- 3oz/75g grated Cheddar cheese
- ½ tbsp olive oil
- Seasoning to taste

Method

1 Heat the olive oil in a large pan, and add diced onions. Sauté until softened on a medium heat.

2 Add the beef, garlic, seasoning, chilli flakes and cumin, continuing to cook until browned. Remove any excess fat.

3 Add the corn and continue to cook through until meat is done.

4 Put to one side whilst you wash the lettuce leaves and gently pat dry. Fill large leaves with a generous spoonful of the beef mixture, before topping with grated cheese. Wrap and enjoy immediately.

Chefs Note....
Add a little fresh salsa or sour cream for extra zing.

Fast Tuna Protein Pot

CLEANSE DETOX & SHRED FAT

Ingredients

- 4oz/125g tuna flakes in spring water, drained
- 2 large eggs, hard boiled and peeled
- Handful of baby spinach leaves

- 5-6 baby plum tomatoes, halved
- 1 tbsp French dressing
- Seasoning to taste

Method

1 Slice the boiled eggs into quarters.

2 Layer spinach leaves, egg, tomato and tuna in a bowl.

3 Pour dressing over the mixture, and add seasoning before serving.

Chefs Note....
Add the dressing just before serving to keep vegetables crisp and fresh.

Chicken and Veggie Stir Fry

CLEANSE DETOX & SHRED FAT

Ingredients

- 1 medium sized skinless chicken breast, sliced
- 1 large pepper, thinly sliced
- 2oz/50g mange tout
- 75g/3oz beansprouts
- 1 small onion, finely sliced
- 2oz/50g mushrooms, sliced
- 1 tbsp olive oil
- ½ tsp grated fresh ginger
- 1 clove garlic, crushed
- ½ tbsp soy sauce

Method

1 Heat oil in a large shallow pan and gently sauté the ginger and garlic.

2 Add chicken pieces and cook until tender.

3 Add vegetables and beansprouts continuing to cook until slightly softened.

4 Stir in soy sauce, tossing well to serve.

Chefs Note....
Try mixing it up with other vegetables for variety.

Chicken Stuffed Pepper

SERVES 1

CLEANSE DETOX & SHRED FAT

Ingredients

- 1 large pepper, halved and de-seeded
- ½ onion, finely sliced
- 7oz/200g lean chicken mince
- 2 cloves garlic, crushed
- 2 tsp olive oil
- 2 tbsp fresh herbs, chopped
- Seasoning, to taste

Method

1 Preheat the oven to 350C/180F/Gas4.

2 In a shallow pan heat the oil and add onions, garlic and chicken, cooking until tender.

3 Add chopped fresh herbs and seasoning.

4 Spoon mixture into the pepper halves, and bake for 20-30 minutes or until the peppers are tender and piping hot.

Chefs Note....
Add a drizzle of dressing or hot sauce for a spicier touch.

31

Aubergine Parmesan

CLEANSE DETOX & SHRED FAT

Ingredients

- 1 large aubergine, sliced lengthways
- 2 large tomatoes, de-seeded and diced.
- 1 tbsp olive oil
- ½ tbsp white wine vinegar
- 1 medium sized onion, finely diced
- 2 cloves garlic, crushed
- 1 tsp dried oregano
- 1 tsp brown sugar (optional)
- 4oz/125g grated cheese
- Seasoning to taste
- Handful of fresh basil leaves

Method

1 Slice aubergine into 1 cm thick slices and heat a grill to a high temperature. Lightly salt aubergine slices and put to one aside.

2 In a deep pan, heat oil and add onion, garlic and oregano, cooking until onions are softened. Add the tomatoes and continue to cook on a low temperature, for 10-15 minutes.

3 Dry any moisture from the aubergine slices. Place on a baking sheet, and grill on both sides until lightly charred. Remove and allow to cool.

4 Preheat the oven to 150 C/300F/Gas2.

5 Add sugar, seasoning and white wine vinegar to tomato sauce, and continue to simmer until reduced by a third.

6 In a baking tray, layer grilled aubergine slices with tomato sauce and cheese, and bake in oven until golden and bubbling.

Chefs Note....
Top with fresh basil leaves, torn and scattered over.

Grilled Chicken and Sesame Broccoli

CLEANSE DETOX & SHRED FAT

Ingredients

- 1 medium sized skinless chicken breast, cut into pieces
- 4oz/125g tenderstem broccoli streams
- ½ tbsp olive oil
- ½ tbsp sesame seed oil
- 2 medium sized spring onions, sliced

- 2 cloves garlic, crushed
- 2 tsp honey
- ½ tsp sesame seeds
- ½ tsp grated ginger
- ¼ cup/60ml chicken broth

Method

1 In a bowl, mix half of the sesame oil, soy sauce and honey. Marinade chicken pieces for 20-30 minutes.

2 Heat the oil in a pan and add spring onions, ginger & garlic and sauté for a few minutes.

3 Add the chicken pieces, marinade, broccoli and chicken broth. Cook until the chicken is tender.

4 Sprinkle sesame seeds and drizzle remaining sesame seed oil.

Chefs Note....
Leave some green spring onion slices to use as a garnish.

Mini Bacon Frittatas

CLEANSE DETOX & SHRED FAT

Ingredients

- 1 large egg
- 2 slices cooked back bacon, chopped
- 2oz/50g grated Cheddar cheese

- ½ tbsp milk
- 1 tsp butter
- Seasoning to taste

Method

1 Preheat the oven to 150C/300F/Gas2.

2 Lightly beat the egg with the milk. Add the chopped bacon pieces, cheese and seasoning.

3 Lightly grease a small, deep baking pan with butter, and pour mixture in.

4 Bake until frittata is risen and golden. Serve hot or cold.

Chefs Note....
These keep well in the fridge – make a large batch for quick lunches.

Avocado & Tuna Cup

SERVES 1

CLEANSE DETOX & SHRED FAT

Ingredients

- 1 medium sized avocado, de-stoned and cut in half
- 175g/6oz tuna, drained
- ¼ tsp smoked paprika
- ¼ pepper, finely diced
- ½ chilli, de-seeded and finely sliced
- Seasoning to taste
- Handful of fresh coriander
- Squeeze of lemon juice

Method

1 Scoop out a little of the avocado from each half section to enlarge the stone hole to double it's size in each half.

2 Combine together the tuna, bell pepper, herbs and the avocado which has been scooped out. Load the tuna mixture back into the avocado halves and serve.

Chefs Note....
Add fresh chopped coriander as a garnish.

Chicken Cobb Salad

CLEANSE DETOX & SHRED FAT

Ingredients

- 1 grilled skinless chicken breast
- 2 slices cooked back bacon
- 2oz/5og blue cheese
- 1 hard-boiled egg
- 5-6 cherry tomatoes

- 3-4 Romaine lettuce leaves
- ½ avocado
- Handful fresh chives
- ½ tbsp vinaigrette
- Seasoning

Method

1 Cut the chicken breast, bacon, egg and avocado into slices.

2 Add halved tomatoes and tear lettuce leaves roughly.

3 Add finely chopped chives and crumbled cheese, and toss lightly with vinaigrette and seasoning.

Chefs Note....
Try replacing the bacon with smoked salmon.

Turnip Fries

CLEANSE DETOX & SHRED FAT

Ingredients

- 2 large turnips
- 1 tbsp rapeseed oil
- 1 tsp garlic powder
- Sea salt
- Ground black pepper

Method

1 Preheat oven to 200C/400F/Gas6.

2 Cut the turnips into chunky fries.

3 Toss in oil, garlic powder and seasoning, and spread onto a lined baking tray.

4 Bake for 40 minutes or until cooked through and golden brown.

Chefs Note....
Serve with steak or grilled chicken.

Sliced Beef 'Rolls'

SERVES 1

CLEANSE DETOX & SHRED FAT

Ingredients

- 3oz/75g roast beef slices
- 3oz/75g cheese slices
- ½ cucumber finely sliced

- 1 tsp mustard
- 1 tsp mayonnaise

Method

1 Add a little mustard or mayonnaise to each slice of beef.

2 Lay some cucumber over the top.

3 Layer with a slice of cheese and roll up each piece to make a little beef 'sushi' style roll.

Chefs Note....
Try adding other fillings and spices for an alternative to sandwiches.

Spicy Marinated Prawn Kebabs

CLEANSE DETOX & SHRED FAT

Ingredients

- 12 very large kings prawns
- 2 red peppers
- 2 red onions
- 2 crushed cloves garlic

- 1 tbsp olive oil
- 1 tbsp lime juice
- 1 tsp chilli flakes
- ½ tbsp soy sauce

Method

1 Combine the oil, lime juice, chilli flakes, soy sauce and garlic together.

2 Marinade the prawn in the garlic mixture for at least 30 minutes.

3 After this time preheat the grill.

4 Cut the peppers into chunky pieces. Slice the onions into eighths.

5 Skewer the onion slices, pepper and prawns leaving the rest of the marinade in the bowl.

6 Coat each kebab with the remaining marinade.

7 Cook under a grill for 10-15 minutes or until the prawns are cooked through.

Chefs Note....
Try adding scallops or other seafood and serving with a salad.

Spicy Marinated Prawn Kebabs

CLEANSE DETOX & SHRED FAT

Ingredients

- 12 very large kings prawns
- 2 red peppers
- 2 red onions
- 2 crushed cloves garlic

- 1 tbsp olive oil
- 1 tbsp lime juice
- 1 tsp chilli flakes
- ½ tbsp soy sauce

Method

1 Combine the oil, lime juice, chilli flakes, soy sauce and garlic together.

2 Marinade the prawn in the garlic mixture for at least 30 minutes.

3 After this time preheat the grill.

4 Cut the peppers into chunky pieces. Slice the onions into eighths.

5 Skewer the onion slices, pepper and prawns leaving the rest of the marinade in the bowl.

6 Coat each kebab with the remaining marinade.

7 Cook under a grill for 10-15 minutes or until the prawns are cooked through.

Chefs Note....
Try adding scallops or other seafood and serving with a salad.

Lemon and Herb Cauliflower Steaks

CLEANSE DETOX & SHRED FAT

Ingredients

- 1 large cauliflower
- 1 tbsp olive oil
- 2 cloves garlic, crushed
- 1 tsp chilli flakes
- 1 tbsp lemon juice
- Sea salt and ground pepper

Method

1 Preheat oven to 200C/400F/Gas6.

2 Slice the widest part of the cauliflower into 2 thick slices each an inch or two thick.

3 Combine all the other ingredients together and brush lightly onto each side of cauliflower 'steaks'.

4 Bake for 40 minutes, turning half way, until golden and tender.

Chefs Note....
This is a great veggie lunch snack. Try serving with turnip fries.

Aubergine Lasagne

CLEANSE DETOX & SHRED FAT

Ingredients

- 2 large aubergines
- 1lb/450g beef/ lamb mince
- 3oz/75g mushrooms
- 400g/14oz tinned chopped tomatoes
- 1 large onion, diced
- 2 tbsp olive oil

- 4oz/125g grated mozzarella cheese
- 3 cloves garlic, crushed
- 1 tsp dried basil
- 1 tsp dried oregano
- Cooking oil spray/ extra olive oil

Method

1 Preheat oven to 170C/350F/Gas4.

2 Heat the oil and add diced onions and garlic, cooking until softened.

3 Add the mince and continue to cook until browned.

4 Using a food processor, mince mushrooms and add to meat. Continue to cook.

5 Add the chopped tomatoes and herbs, and cook until sauce is thickened and reduced.

6 Slice aubergines thinly lengthways, into pieces 3-4 mm thick. Spray with cooking oil or lightly brush olive oil on top.

7 In a baking tray, layer aubergine slices with sauce. Once completed, add mozzarella on top.

8 Cook for 30-40 minutes until sauce is bubbling at edges and everything is tender and cooked through.

Chefs Note....
Top with fresh torn basil leaves.

Portobello Mushroom Burger

Ingredients

- 2 Portobello Mushrooms
- 1 red onion
- 1 large tomato
- 2oz/50g sliced cheese
- ½ avocado
- Sea salt and black pepper
- Olive oil

Method

1 Preheat oven to 170C/350F/Gas4.

2 Remove stems from mushrooms and lightly brush with olive oil.

3 Cook in oven until brown and tender on both sides.

4 Peel the avocado and add salt and pepper. Mash lightly.

5 Once mushrooms are cooked, layer with slices of tomato, onions, cheese and avocado spread.

Chefs Note....
Add crispy fried bacon for extra crunch and flavour.

Crispy Bacon and Courgetti

CLEANSE DETOX & SHRED FAT

Ingredients

- 2 large courgettes
- 2 slices back bacon, cut into small pieces
- 1 tbsp chickpea flour
- 1 egg white
- Seasoning
- Olive oil for frying
- Water as required

Method

1 Slice the courgettes into fine matchstick pieces. Sprinkle with salt and leave for a few minutes under layers of kitchen towel to absorb the moisture.

2 Prepare the batter by mixing the flour & seasoning and slowly beating an egg white into mixture. Add a little water, until the mixture reaches a paste consistency of medium thickness.

3 Add the courgette pieces and combine until well coated.

4 Heat the oil in a shallow pan, and add handfuls of courgette, cooking for 2-3 minutes until crispy and golden.

5 Fry bacon pieces until crispy. Combine with courgette and serve.

Chefs Note....
This is great as a main or a side dish which you can serve with grilled fish or meat.

Soy and Ginger Glazed Scallops

CLEANSE DETOX & SHRED FAT

Ingredients

- 6 fresh scallops
- 1 tbsp lemon juice
- 1 tsp fresh grated ginger
- 2 cloves garlic, crushed
- 1 tsp honey
- 1 tbsp soy sauce
- Olive oil

Method

1 Mix the honey, lemon, ginger, garlic and soy together. Remove a third of the mixture, and use this to marinade scallops for 20-30 minutes.

2 Brush scallops lightly with olive oil and cook under a grill or on a skewer for 2-3 minutes each side, adding the extra glaze sauce while cooking.

3 Serve immediately.

Chefs Note....
Serve with steamed sugar snap peas.

Stuffed Tomato Courgette

CLEANSE DETOX & SHRED FAT

Ingredients

- 4 large courgettes
- 1lb/450g turkey mince
- 3oz/75g mushrooms
- 400g/14oz tinned chopped tomatoes
- 3 cloves garlic, crushed

- 1 tsp dried basil
- 1 tsp dried oregano
- 1 large onion
- 2 tbsp olive oil
- 4oz/125g mozzarella ball, cut into slices

Method

1 Preheat oven to 170C/350F/Gas4.

2 Heat the oil and add diced onions and garlic, cooking until softened.

3 Add mince and continue to cook through.

4 Add chopped tomatoes and herbs, and cook until sauce thickens. Remove from heat.

5 Cut courgettes in half lengthways, scooping out insides.

6 Add meat sauce into each courgette section, topping with slices of cheese.

7 Cook for 20 minutes or until courgette halves are tender.

Chefs Note....
Top with fresh herbs.

low carb
dinner
recipes

LOSE WEIGHT FOR GOOD
LOW CARB DIET FOR BEGINNERS

Spinach and Cheese Savoury Waffles

SERVES 2

CLEANSE DETOX & SHRED FAT

Ingredients

- 2½oz/60g almond flour
- 2oz/ 50g grated cheese
- 2 medium eggs
- ½ cup/120ml milk
- 1 tbsp oil

- Handful of fresh spinach leaves
- ½ tsp baking powder
- Salt and ground pepper to taste
- cooking oil spray

Method

1 Mix the wet ingredients in a large bowl.

2 Slowly sift in the flour and baking powder, and blend.

3 Add the cheese and seasoning, stirring into mixture.

4 Chop the spinach leaves roughly, adding to waffle mixture

5 Cook in a waffle maker according to instructions.

6 Serve immediately, or cool and store for later.

Chefs Note....
Top with a poached egg and smoked salmon or bacon.

SERVES 4

Cheese and Broccoli Bake

CLEANSE DETOX & SHRED FAT

Ingredients

- 2 large heads of broccoli
- 12 large eggs
- 8oz/225g grated cheese

- 2 tbsp milk
- Ground black pepper

Method

1 Preheat oven to 175C/350F/Gas4.

2 Cut the broccoli into small bite size florets and steam until just tender.

3 Break the eggs into a large bowl, adding milk and seasoning.

4 Layer the steamed broccoli florets in a large oven-proof dish, adding cheese on top. Pour egg mixture over the cheese, and bake for 25 minutes, or until golden brown and firm at the top.

5 Delicious served hot or cold.

Chefs Note....
Add a spoonful of sour cream for a creamy touch.

Spiced Beef Roast

CLEANSE DETOX & SHRED FAT

Ingredients

- 3lb/1.35 kg best beef joint
- 2 tbsp Worcestershire Sauce
- 2 tbsp tomato puree
- 2 tbsp bacon fat or coconut oil
- 1 cup/250ml beef stock

- 2 tsp ground cumin
- 1 tsp ground chilli
- 1 tsp garlic powder
- 1 tsp ground coriander
- Seasoning to taste

Method

1 Preheat oven to 140C/275F/Gas1.

2 Season the beef joint in the dry spices and seasoning.

3 In a large tin add the bacon fat and heat over the hob until very hot.

4 Add the beef joint and quickly brown on all sides.

5 Whisk together the broth, Worcestershire sauce and tomato puree then pour over the meat. Bring to boil over the hob and simmer for 30 minutes.

6 Cook in the oven for at least 6-8 hours until cooked to your liking.

Chefs Note....
You can also use a slow cooker instead of an oven.

Low Carb Shepherd's Pie

CLEANSE DETOX & SHRED FAT

Ingredients

- 1 large cauliflower
- 1lb/450g lean beef mince
- 1 large onion, finely diced
- 3½oz/100g button mushrooms, sliced
- 400g/14oz tinned chopped tomatoes
- 2 tbsp olive oil
- 4oz/125g grated cheese
- 1 tbsp butter

- 1 tbsp double cream
- ¼ cup/60ml beef stock
- 2 cloves garlic
- 1 tsp dried rosemary
- 1 tsp thyme
- ½ tbsp Worcestershire sauce
- Seasoning to taste

Method

1 Preheat oven to 180C/350F/Gas4.

2 Heat the olive oil in a saucepan and sauté the onions until softened.

3 Add the crushed garlic and continue to cook for a few minutes.

4 Add the beef and cook until it is browned.

5 Add the mushrooms, herbs, Worcestershire sauce, stock and tinned tomatoes. Continue to cook on a low heat, until most of the liquid evaporates.

6 Cut the cauliflower into small pieces. Steam until cooked and soft. Leave aside to cool for a little while.

7 Once cooled, add butter, cream and seasoning then puree until smooth.

8 Empty the cooked meat in a large oven-proof tray, and top with the cauliflower mix.

9 Add the grated cheese on top and bake for 30 minutes, until the cheese has browned.

Chefs Note....
Make a large batch and store for a quick and easy ready-made dinner.

Cheesy Ham and Cauliflower

CLEANSE DETOX & SHRED FAT

Ingredients

- 1 large cauliflower
- 4oz/125g chopped cooked ham
- 1 cup/250ml double cream
- 5oz/150g grated cheese
- 1 tbsp butter
- 1 onion, finely sliced

- ½ tbsp olive oil
- 1 tsp dried thyme
- ½ tsp cayenne pepper
- ½ tsp garlic powder
- ½ tsp ground nutmeg

Method

1 Preheat oven to 180C/350F/Gas4.

2 Sauté the onion in a saucepan with olive oil for a few minutes.

3 Add the chopped ham and continue to cook for a further 3-4 minutes, then leave aside.

4 Cut the cauliflower into small pieces and steam until cooked.

5 Melt the butter in a separate pan, adding dry herbs and seasoning. Once mixed add cream, stirring until well mixed. Add half of the cheese, stirring in well.

6 Mix the cauliflower, ham and cheese sauce together.

7 Pour into a casserole dish.

8 Top with remaining cheese and bake for a few minutes until golden brown on top.

Chefs Note....
Serve with a crisp green salad.

Thai Coconut Chicken Curry

CLEANSE DETOX & SHRED FAT

Ingredients

- 1 onion, chopped
- 1 red pepper, deseeded & sliced
- 1lb/450g chicken breast, chopped
- 500ml/2 cups coconut milk
- 1 tbsp coconut oil
- 9oz/250g green beans
- 1 juiced lime
- 2-3 curry leaves
- 2 tbsp Thai curry paste
- Handful fresh coriander

Method

1 Heat the coconut oil in a pan and sauté the onions and peppers for a few minutes.

2 Add the curry leaves, Thai paste and chicken, stirring until fragrant.

3 Pour in coconut milk and add the beans and lime juice. Continue to cook until the beans are tender and the chicken is cooked through.

Chefs Note....
Top with fresh chopped coriander.

Chicken and Leek Pie

CLEANSE DETOX & SHRED FAT

Ingredients

- 1lb/450g chicken breast diced
- 7oz/200g cream cheese
- 1 tbsp butter
- 3 medium leeks, sliced finely
- 1 tsp thyme
- Seasoning to taste

Pastry crust:
- 2½oz/ 60g almond flour
- 2½oz/60g coconut flour
- 2 eggs
- 2 tbsp butter
- ½ tsp salt

Method

1 Gently heat the butter in a saucepan and sauté the leeks until softened.

2 Add the chicken pieces, cooking until browned.

3 Add cream cheese, stirring until softened.

4 Add grated cheese, thyme and seasoning, continuing to stir. Empty into a pie dish.

5 Form pastry crust by mixing the flours and salt together.

6 Melt the butter and mix into dry ingredients, kneading until crumbs form.

7 Add the eggs and a splash of milk if needed, until a dough forms.

8 Roll out, and place on top of filling. Prick with a fork, and bake in oven for 30 minutes or until golden.

Chefs Note....
Serve with a fresh salad.

Courgette Noodles and Meatballs

CLEANSE DETOX & SHRED FAT

Ingredients

- 1lb/450g turkey mince
- 2oz/50g grated Parmesan cheese
- Handful fresh chopped parsley
- 2 eggs
- 1 tbsp ground almonds
- 1 large onion, finely chopped
- 2 cloves crushed garlic
- 2 tbsp olive oil

- 4 large courgettes
- 400g/14oz tinned chopped tomatoes
- 1 tbsp Balsamic vinegar
- ½ tsp dried oregano
- ½ tsp dried basil
- ½ tsp chilli flakes
- 1 tbsp Worcestershire sauce
- Seasoning to taste

Method

1 Combine the turkey mince, ground almonds, parsley, seasoning, cheese and eggs in a large bowl and form into even balls.

2 Heat a little olive oil in a frying pan and add meatballs. Cook until golden. Remove and leave aside.

3 Add the remaining oil, chopped onions and crushed garlic, cooking until softened.

4 Add the chopped tomatoes, seasoning, herbs, Balsamic vinegar and Worcestershire sauce. Cook on a medium heat until half of the liquid begins to evaporate.

5 Using a spiralizer, form noodles from the courgettes. Add meatballs to sauce, cooking for a few minutes. Add courgette noodles just before serving, cooking for a minute or two until tender.

Chefs Note....
Keep raw courgette noodles separate until ready to serve.

Roasted Lemon Chicken and Broccoli

CLEANSE
DETOX &
SHRED FAT

Ingredients

- 1lb/450g chicken breast diced
- 7oz/200g cream cheese
- 1 tbsp butter
- 3 medium leeks, sliced finely
- 1 tsp thyme
- Seasoning to taste

Pastry crust:
- 2 ½oz/60g almond flour
- 2½oz/60g coconut flour
- 2 eggs
- 2 tbsp butter
- ½ tsp salt

Method

1 Preheat oven to 180C/350F/Gas4.

2 Heat the butter in a frying pan, add the leeks and cook until softened.

3 Add the chicken, cooking until browned.

4 Add the cream cheese and stir until softened.

5 Add thyme and seasoning, continuing to stir then empty into a pie dish.

6 Form pastry crust by the mixing flours and salt together.

7 Melt the butter and mix into dry ingredients, kneading until crumbs form.

8 Add the eggs and a splash of milk if needed, until a dough forms.

9 Roll out, and place on top of filling. Prick with a fork, and bake in oven for 30 minutes or until golden.

Chefs Note....
Serve with a fresh salad.

Grilled Chicken Salad

CLEANSE DETOX & SHRED FAT

Ingredients

- 1 grilled chicken breast
- 1 small avocado
- 3-4 romaine lettuce leaves
- 5-6 cherry tomatoes
- ½ tbsp chopped hazelnuts
- 1 dill pickle, sliced

- ¼ cucumber, sliced
- 2oz/50g feta cheese, crumbled
- handful of rocket leaves
- Olive oil for drizzling
- Seasoning to taste

Method

1 Sliced the grilled chicken into small slices.

2 De-stone and slice avocado, cucumber, dill & tomatoes and combine in a bowl with chicken.

3 Tear romaine leaves and add to bowl, along with rocket leaves.

4 Add the chopped nuts and feta cheese.

5 Drizzle with oil, add seasoning and toss lightly before serving.

Chefs Note....
Ideal for using up leftover chicken.

Roasted Mozzarella Aubergine

CLEANSE DETOX & SHRED FAT

Ingredients

- 2 large aubergines
- 4oz/125g mozzarella
- 2 large beef tomatoes, sliced
- Olive oil to drizzle
- Sea salt and ground pepper
- Fresh basil leaves

Method

1 Preheat the oven to 170C/325F/Gas3.

2 Cut the aubergines in half lengthways and place on a baking tray.

3 Drizzle with a little olive oil, and bake for 20-30 minutes until the flesh is softened.

4 Remove from oven. Top with slices of mozzarella and tomato and sprinkle with sea salt and pepper.

5 Bake for a further 10 minutes or until the cheese has melted.

6 Top with fresh basil leaves and serve.

Chefs Note....
Add chilli flakes for a kick of heat.

Steamed Foil Lemon Fish

CLEANSE DETOX & SHRED FAT

Ingredients

- 4 large boneless white fish fillets
- 1 whole lemon, sliced
- 4 cloves garlic, crushed
- Ground black pepper

- 4 tsp garlic butter
- ½ tbsp lemon juice
- Olive oil for drizzling

Method

1 Preheat oven to 180C/350F/Gas4.

2 Place the fillets on a piece of foil each.

3 Mix the garlic, butter and lemon juice into a paste. Spread lightly over each piece of fish.

4 Place lemon slices on top and add ground black pepper. Drizzle a little olive oil over each piece of fish.

5 Fold up lightly closed foil parcels, and bake for 15 minutes or until the fish is cooked through. Serve immediately.

Chefs Note....
Serve with a steamed green beans or salad.

Spicy Soy Salmon and Noodles

CLEANSE DETOX & SHRED FAT

Ingredients

- 2 large fillets of salmon
- 2 large courgettes
- 2 tsp fresh grated ginger
- 2 cloves garlic crushed
- ½ - 1 tsp chilli flakes
- 2 tsp honey

- 1 tbsp soy sauce
- 1 tbsp sesame seed oil
- Sea salt
- Ground black pepper
- Cooking oil spray

Method

1 Mix together ginger, garlic, chilli flakes, soy, honey and sesame seed oil in a large bowl to make a marinade.

2 Brush the salmon fillets with a little of the marinade.

3 Add cooking oil spray to a pan, and cook the salmon fillets, turning until almost cooked through. Pour the remaining marinade on top and keep on a low heat until sauce begins to thicken a little. Remove from heat, and remove salmon from the pan.

4 Use a spiralizer to make noodles from each courgette. Toss them lightly in the remaining sauce until coated. Top with ground black pepper and serve.

Chefs Note....
Add toasted sesame seeds for an extra crunch.

Creamy Red Pepper Soup

SERVES 2

CLEANSE DETOX & SHRED FAT

Ingredients

- 2 large red peppers, deseeded & halved
- 3 cloves garlic, crushed
- 1 large onion, finely sliced
- 2 sticks celery, finely sliced
- 1 tbsp olive oil
- 2 cups/500ml chicken or vegetable stock
- 1 cup/250ml single cream
- 2 oz/50g grated cheese
- Seasoning to taste

Method

1 Brush the peppers with oil and place under a preheated grill until charred all over. Make sure to turn regularly.

2 Leave aside in a covered bowl to cool and cut pepper into pieces.

3 Heat the olive oil in a pan and add the onions, garlic and celery, cooking until softened. Add pepper and stock, heating until it begins to boil.

4 Remove from heat. Using a blender, process until the mixture is smooth. Return back to the pan. Keep on a low heat and add the cream, cheese and seasoning until wormed through.

Chefs Note....
Serve with a drizzle of cream on top.

Spinach & Ricotta Frittata

CLEANSE DETOX & SHRED FAT

Ingredients

- 6 large eggs
- 1 large white onion
- 3½oz/100g ricotta cheese
- 3½oz/100g baby spinach

- 7oz/200g cherry tomatoes, halved
- 2oz/50g grated cheese
- 1 tbsp olive oil

Method

1 Preheat oven to 180C/350F/Gas4.

2 In a small square oven-proof dish, heat olive oil and add the diced onions. Cook until softened.

3 Add the tomatoes, cooking until slightly softened.

4 Beat the eggs and add grated cheese & spinach leaves, mixing in.

5 Pour the eggs over onions, stirring slightly to keep tomatoes and spinach even throughout. Remove from heat.

6 Add spoonful's of ricotta across the mixture and cook in oven until golden browned and the eggs are firm on top.

Chefs Note....
Serve with a crisp green salad.

Roast Vegetable Pizza

SERVES 2

CLEANSE DETOX & SHRED FAT

Ingredients

- 2 large onions
- 2 large red peppers
- 4oz/125g portabello mushrooms
- 2oz/50g broccoli florets
- 2oz/50g asparagus spears
- 2oz/50g baby spinach leaves
- 4oz/125g ricotta cheese
- 2oz/50g cherry tomatoes
- 1 tbsp olive oil

- Sea salt and ground pepper

For base:
- 12 egg whites
- 2 tsp baking powder
- ½ tsp dried basil
- ½ tsp chilli flakes
- 1 tsp salt
- 1 oz/25g coconut flour
- Cooking oil spray

Method

1 Slice onions, tomatoes and large vegetables.

2 Prepare the base by beating the egg whites for a couple of minutes, then add the flour, baking powder and spices.

3 Heat a large flat frying pan and add a little cooking oil spray. Add half the base mixture, spreading thinly. Cook for 2-3 minutes and flip to cook other side. Remove the cooked base and make another base with the remaining mixture.

4 Preheat oven to 170C/325F/Gas3.

5 Arrange all the vegetables across the two bases

Add scoops of ricotta cheese across them evenly. Drizzle olive oil and add seasoning.

6 Bake for 20-30 minutes or until vegetables are tender. Serve immediately.

Chefs Note....
The base also makes a great low carb flat bread option.

Tandoori Marinated Chicken Curry

CLEANSE DETOX & SHRED FAT

Ingredients

- 4 skinless chicken breasts, diced
- 4 tbsp Greek style natural yoghurt
- 2 tsp chilli flakes
- 2 tsp ground turmeric
- 2 tbsp ground coriander
- 2 tbsp ground cumin

- 1 tsp fresh grated ginger
- 2 cloves garlic, crushed
- 1 tbsp lemon juice
- 2 dried bay leaves
- 2 tbsp olive oil
- Seasoning to taste

Method

1 Mix all powdered spices, ginger and crushed garlic together with lemon juice. Add the yoghurt, stirring until well mixed. Add salt to season as required.

2 Add the chicken pieces and marinade for at least 2-4 hours, or longer if possible.

3 Heat the oil in a large pan, and add bay leaves, cooking until fragrant.

4 Add the chicken pieces and remaining marinade. Cook for 30-40 minutes on a medium heat, until chicken is tender.

Chefs Note....
Serve with low carb flatbread, salad and mango chutney.

Slow Cooker Turkey Stuffed Peppers

SERVES 2

CLEANSE DETOX & SHRED FAT

Ingredients

- 4 large red peppers
- 1 large onion, chopped
- 1 lb/450g turkey mince
- 1 small cauliflower
- 4oz/125g grated cheese
- 2 cloves garlic, crushed

- 2 tbsp olive oil
- 2 tsp dried oregano
- 2 tsp dried basil
- 1 tsp chilli flakes
- Sea salt

Method

1 Heat oil in a large pan and add the chopped onions and garlic. Cook until softened.

2 Add the mince, continuing to cook until browned. Add salt and dry herbs and continue to cook until cooked through. Remove from heat.

3 In a food processor, chop cauliflower until it is becomes crumbs.

4 Combine the cauliflower crumbs with the cooked turkey meat and cheese, mixing well.

5 Remove the tops from each bell pepper, deseed and put to one aside.

6 Use a spoon to carefully add turkey mixture inside each pepper then cover with the top part of pepper.

7 Place peppers inside a slow cooker, and cook on a medium heat for 3-4 hours or until tender.

Chefs Note....
For a vegetarian take, replace meat with minced mushrooms.

Shakshuka

CLEANSE DETOX & SHRED FAT

Ingredients

- 3-4 large eggs
- 1 onion, diced
- 1 red pepper, diced
- 3oz/75g spinach
- 200g/7oz chopped tomatoes
- 1 tbsp tomato puree
- 3 cloves garlic, crushed

- ½ tsp cumin seeds
- 1 tsp paprika
- ½ tsp cayenne pepper
- ½ tsp oregano
- ½ tbsp Worcestershire sauce
- Fresh chopped coriander
- Seasoning

Method

1 Heat oil in a large pan. Add the diced onions, garlic and cumin seeds, cooking until the onions have softened.

2 Add the peppers and continue to cook. Add remaining dry spices and stir.

3 Stir in the chopped tomatoes, tomato puree and seasoning, and cook until oil bubbles start to appear on top and sauce has slightly reduced. Reduce heat to low.

4 Add spinach leaves, cooking until slightly wilted.

5 Crack the eggs on top, keeping yolks intact.

6 Cover pan and continue to cook until eggs are from, serve immediately.

Chefs Note....
Garnish with fresh chopped coriander.

low carb
snack
recipes

LOSE
WEIGHT
FOR GOOD
LOW CARB DIET
FOR BEGINNERS

Low Carb Rice-Free Sushi

SERVES 16-20

CLEANSE DETOX & SHRED FAT

Ingredients

- 4oz/125g smoked salmon
- 1 medium sized pepper
- ½ cucumber

- ½ large avocado
- 4-5 large sushi seaweed sheets

Method

1 Prepare the filling by slicing smoked salmon and vegetables into long, thin strips, roughly the width of one seaweed sheet.

2 Place strips in one row along a sheet. Wet the furthest end of the sheet, and slowly roll into a tight shape, pressing the wet end down lightly, to help it seal.

3 Continue until all the filling and sheets have been used.

4 Slice into small pieces with a sharp, slightly wet knife.

Chefs Note....
Try different crisp vegetables such as celery or carrot, to add colour and flavour.

Cabbage Spring Rolls

CLEANSE DETOX & SHRED FAT

Ingredients

- 1 large white cabbage
- 1 medium sized white onion, finely diced
- 1lb 2oz/500g lean minced turkey meat
- 2 large carrots, grated

- 2-3 cloves garlic, crushed
- 1 tsp ginger, grated
- 1 tbsp olive oil
- Cooking oil spray

Method

1 Carefully remove cabbage leaves, keeping them whole. Lay in a steaming tray and cook in a steamer until wilted. Remove and allow to cool.

2 Preheat the oven to 160C/325F/Gas3.

3 In a medium sized pan add the olive oil and gently fry the onions until they begin to soften. Add the garlic and ginger, followed by turkey meat and cook for a few minutes until cooked through.

4 Stir in grated carrots. Add a spoonful of mixture in the centre of each cabbage leaf, and roll into a spring roll shape.

5 Assemble rolls on a baking tray, and spray lightly with cooking oil. Bake for 15-20 minutes until crispy, turning once. Serve immediately.

Chefs Note....
Add some chopped fresh chilli to the rolls for a little spice.

Easy Energy Bites

SERVES 10

Ingredients

- 3oz/75g almond butter
- 2oz/50g dried coconut flakes
- 1 tbsp coconut oil

- 1 tbsp pure cocoa powder
- 1 tbsp ground almond meal
- Stevia or alternative sweetener to taste

Method

1 Combine all ingredients in a food processor until well combined.

2 Remove mixture into a large bowl. Form into 10 portions and roll into round shapes.

3 Store in an airtight container and keep refrigerated.

Chefs Note....
Try adding cinnamon or using different nut butters for a different flavour.

Crust-free Bitesize Quiches

CLEANSE DETOX & SHRED FAT

Ingredients

- 6 medium sized eggs
- 2 medium sized tomatoes, diced
- 3oz/75g smoked salmon, cut into small pieces.

- 2oz/50g grated cheese
- Salt & pepper to taste

Method

1 Preheat oven to 160C/325F/Gas3.

2 Beat the eggs in a large bowl.

3 Add diced tomatoes, salmon and cheese. Add seasoning as required.

4 Pour mixture into 6 silicon muffin moulds. Place in a muffin tray and bake until golden and risen.

5 Remove and cool. Keep refrigerated until serving.

Chefs Note....
Add a handful of fresh chopped herbs for an extra touch.

Gluten-free Scotch Eggs

CLEANSE DETOX & SHRED FAT

Ingredients

- 9 large eggs
- 1lb/ 500g beef or pork mince
- 4oz /125g ground almonds
- Seasoning to taste

Method

1 Preheat oven to 180C/350F/Gas4.

2 Hard boil 8 eggs. Once cooked and cooled, peel the eggs and put to one side.

3 Season the meat. Divide into 8 portions, and form a small, round patty with each portion.

4 Place each boiled egg at the centre of each patty, carefully wrapping over the egg to encase each egg individually in the meat patty.

5 Beat the remaining egg in a bowl. Lightly dip each covered egg and roll in ground almonds until coated.

6 Place covered eggs on a baking tray, and cook for 15-20mins or until golden brown and cooked through

7 Cool and store in a refrigerator.

Chefs Note....
Add fresh herbs or spices to the meat mix for a spicier taste.

Chocolate Chip Cookies

CLEANSE DETOX & SHRED FAT

Ingredients

- 1 large egg
- 11oz/300g almond flour
- 3oz/75g unsalted butter
- 3oz/75g dark chocolate chips
- 3oz/75g sweetener (stevia or similar)
- 1 tsp vanilla extract

Method

1 Preheat oven to 180C/350F/Gas4.

2 In a large bowl combine the butter and sweetener until it becomes lightly fluffy.

3 Combine egg and vanilla extract, and slowly add almond flour until it is a smooth, thick mixture.

4 Fold in chocolate chips.

5 Divide mixture into approx. 15 or more round spoonful's on a baking tray. Bake for 10-15 minutes until lightly golden.

6 Allow to cool before storing away.

Chefs Note....
Add a handful of chopped nuts for extra crunch.

Baked Courgette Crisps

CLEANSE
DETOX &
SHRED FAT

Ingredients

- 1 large courgette
- Cooking oil spray
- Salt & Pepper to taste
- Sprinkle of paprika

Method

1 Preheat oven to 140C/275F/Gas1.

2 Slice an unpeeled courgette into thin slices using a mandolin slicer.

3 Place on a baking tray and spray lightly with cooking oil.

4 Add a little seasoning and paprika and bake in oven for approx. 60 minutes, turning half way until crisp and dry.

5 Eat within a few hours to keep their crunchy texture.

Chefs Note....
Experiment with different seasonings for a variety of flavours.

Spicy Cauliflower Bites

CLEANSE DETOX & SHRED FAT

Ingredients

- 1 large cauliflower head
- 4oz/125g almond flour
- 1 large egg
- 1 tsp cumin

- 1 tsp garlic powder
- 1 tsp chilli flakes
- 1 tsp dried ginger powder
- 1 tsp dried mango powder (optional)

Method

1 Preheat oven to 200C/400F/Gas6.

2 Cut up cauliflower into large bite size florets.

3 Lightly beat the egg and coat each cauliflower piece in egg.

4 Combine the spices and almond flour in a large dish.

5 Toss the cauliflower pieces in flour mixture and place on baking tray.

6 Bake for 25 minutes, or until browned and tender.

Chefs Note....
Mix up a dip with Greek yoghurt and spices for the perfect partner.

SERVES 2

Tuna Topped Cucumber Floats

CLEANSE DETOX & SHRED FAT

Ingredients

- 1 large cucumber
- 1 tin tuna in spring water, drained
- 75g/3oz soft cheese
- Ground black pepper to taste
- Fresh dill, to taste

Method

1 Combine the tuna, soft cheese, herbs and seasoning in a bowl.

2 Cut the cucumber into half, and cut each section lengthways to make 4 pieces in total.

3 With a teaspoon, carefully scoop out seeds and pulp, leaving the firmer flesh and skin of the 4 pieces.

4 Add the tuna mixture to each section and serve.

Chefs Note....
Top with a little fresh dill as a garnish.

No Bake Rocky Road Bites

CLEANSE DETOX & SHRED FAT

Ingredients

- 7oz/200g dark chocolate
- 2 tbsp peanut butter
- 2oz/50g coarsely chopped almonds
- 2oz/50g freeze dried raspberries

Method

1 In a glass bowl placed over a pan of hot water, carefully melt chocolate until smooth.

2 Stir in the peanut butter, mixing until even.

3 Add the almonds and raspberries and pour the mixture into a lined shallow tray. Refrigerate for 1 hour until slightly firm.

4 Remove and score into slices.

5 Refrigerate for an additional hour, then separate into slices and store cold.

Chefs Note....
Use a few extra nuts and berries and grind finely to add as a colourful topping before cooling.

low carb
dessert
recipes

Chocolate Mousse

CLEANSE DETOX & SHRED FAT

Ingredients

- 2oz/50g soft cheese
- 3½floz/100ml whipping cream

- 2oz/50g dark chocolate
- ½ tsp sweetener (stevia or similar)

Method

1 In a glass bowl, break chocolate into pieces and melt slowly over a pan of hot water.

2 Once melted put to one side.

3 Whip the cream, adding sweetener, until thick, fluffy peaks form. Start to beat in soft cheese until blended. Slowly fold in the melted chocolate until evenly mixed.

4 Refrigerate for at least 1 hour or longer, and serve.

Chefs Note....
Use darker chocolate for a more intense and rich taste.

New York Cheesecake

CLEANSE DETOX & SHRED FAT

Ingredients

Filling:
- 2lb/900g soft cheese
- 3½floz/ 100ml double cream
- 2 tbsp sweetener (stevia or similar)
- 4 eggs
- 1 tsp vanilla extract

Crust:
- 9oz/250g almonds
- 3 tbsp butter
- 1 tbsp sweetener (stevia or similar)

Method

1 Preheat oven to 180C/350f/Gas4.

2 Grease a round spring-form tin.

3 Beat the cream cheese, eggs and cream together. Add the sweetener and vanilla extract.

4 Make filling by mixing almonds, butter and remaining sweetener in a food processor, until it starts to stick to the side.

5 Add the filling to tin. Pour the cheese filling on top and bake for 45-50 minutes, or until top is set. Cool completely before serving.

Chefs Note....
Serve with fresh berries.

No Churn Vanilla Ice cream

SERVES 10

CLEANSE DETOX & SHRED FAT

Ingredients

- 2 cups/500ml double cream
- 1½oz/40g vanilla protein powder

- Seeds from 1 vanilla pod
- 3 tbsp sweetener (stevia or similar)

Method

1 Whip double cream until peaks start to form. Beat in the protein powder, sweetener and vanilla.

2 Pour into a container and freeze for at least 3 hours, removing every 30 minutes to lightly stir.

Chefs Note....
Try other flavours by adding flavoured protein powders or cocoa for a chocolate version.

Pecan Pie

CLEANSE DETOX & SHRED FAT

Ingredients

- 2 large eggs
- 1 cup/250ml sugar free syrup
- 6oz/175g pecan nuts
- 2 tbsp sweetener (stevia or similar)
- 2 tbsp butter
- 1 tsp vanilla extract

Crust:
- 3oz/75g almond flour
- 3oz/75g coconut flour
- 2 eggs
- 2 tbsp sweetener
- 2 tbsp butter
- ½ tsp salt

Method

1 Preheat oven to 180C/350F/Gas4.

2 Form a pastry crust by sifting the flour, sweetener and salt together.

3 Melt butter and mix into dry ingredients, kneading together until a dough forms.

4 Roll out, and press into a greased shallow pastry tin.

5 Spread pecan pieces over the pastry shell.

6 Beat the eggs, syrup, sweetener, butter and vanilla and pour on top.

7 Bake for 40 minutes. Allow to cool at room temperature before serving.

Chefs Note....
Serve with a spoonful of vanilla ice cream.

Blueberry Tart

CLEANSE DETOX & SHRED FAT

Ingredients

- 8oz/ 250g soft cheese
- 1 cup/ 250ml whipping cream
- 2 tbsp sweetener (stevia or similar)
- 1 tsp lemon juice
- 3½oz/100g fresh blueberries

Crust:
- 9 0z/250g almonds
- 3 tbsp butter
- 1 tbsp sweetener

Method

1 Preheat oven to 150C/300F/Gas3.

2 Prepare the crust by combining the almonds, butter and sweetener in a food processor. Press the mixture into a shallow pan tray and bake until golden.

3 Remove and leave to cool.

4 Whip the cream until light and fluffy. Add the sweetener, soft cheese and lemon juice. Spoon the cream mixture into cooled pastry shell and top with fresh blueberries. Leave in refrigerator until ready to serve.

Chefs Note....
As an alternative, fold blueberries into the filling.

Raspberry Swirl No Bake Mini Cheesecake

CLEANSE DETOX & SHRED FAT

Ingredients

- Filling:
- 9oz/250g soft cheese
- 1 cup/250ml whipping cream
- 2 tbsp sweetener (stevia or similar)
- 1 tsp lemon juice
- 4oz/125g fresh raspberries
- ¼ tsp xanthan gum

- Crust:
- 3oz/ 75g walnuts
- 2oz/ 50g almond meal
- 2 tbsp butter
- 1 tsp sweetener (stevia or similar)
- 1 tsp cinnamon

Method

1 Whip the soft cheese and cream together until light and fluffy. Add 1½ tbsp of the sweetener and lemon juice, blending together lightly.

2 Prepare the crust by combining all the ingredients in a food processor. Press into a shallow bowl, and refrigerate.

3 Puree the raspberries, adding a tbsp of water and the remaining sweetener. Stir in xanthan gum.

4 Pour the raspberry mixture over cheese filling, and gently form swirls with a knife blade.

5 Refrigerate for at least 2 hours, and serve.

Chefs Note....
Leave a little raspberry sauce aside to serve on top.

Hazelnut Chocolate Truffle Bites

MAKES 10-12

**CLEANSE
DETOX &
SHRED FAT**

Ingredients

- 11oz/300g hazelnuts
- 3oz/75g sugar free dark chocolate
- 3 tbsp almond butter

- 1oz 25g unsweetened cocoa powder
- 1oz/25g sweetener (stevia or similar)
- 1 tsp vanilla extract

Method

1 Chop the hazelnuts in a food processor and put aside 2 tbsp of chopped nuts.

2 Add the almond butter, cocoa powder, sweetener and vanilla extract. Blend until smooth and well combined. Form into 20-12 small round balls.

3 Melt the chocolate pieces in a bowl. Dip the butter balls in molten chocolate and roll lightly in remaining nuts.

4 Store in refrigerator.

Chefs Note....
The truffle mixture also makes
a perfect low carb chocolate
hazelnut spread.

Peanut Butter Chocolate Bars

CLEANSE DETOX & SHRED FAT

Ingredients

- 6oz/175g peanut butter
- 8oz/225g almond meal
- 4oz/125g butter

- 2 tbsp sweetener (stevia or similar)
- 3½oz/100g sugar-free dark chocolate
- 1 tbsp coconut butter

Method

1 Combine the peanut butter, butter, sweetener and almond meal in a food processor until mixed. Empty into a lined shallow tray.

2 Melt chocolate in a bowl and add coconut butter, stirring well and pour this over the peanut butter mix in the tin.

3 Refrigerate for at least 2 hours, and slice into pieces. Store in refrigerator.

Chefs Note....
These can be frozen ahead of time.

Low Carb Eton Mess

CLEANSE DETOX & SHRED FAT

Ingredients

- 6 egg whites
- 4oz/125g sweetener (stevia or similar)
- 1 tsp vanilla extract
- ½ tsp Cream of Tartar
- 1 cup/250ml whipping cream

- 3oz/75g fresh raspberries
- 3oz/75g fresh blueberries
- 20z/50g sugar-free dark chocolate
- ½ tbsp coconut butter

Method

1 Pre-heat oven to 150C/300F/Gas2.

2 Beat the egg whites until stiff peaks start to form. Add the Cream of Tartar and continue to blend.

3 Slowly add the sweetener to egg whites, continuing to mix until they are shiny and glossy.

4 Spread the mixture out onto a baking tray, forming a thick layer. Bake for 60-90 minutes, or until the meringue shell is slightly golden and crisp. Remove and allow to cool.

5 Whisk whipping cream until thick and fluffy. Prepare the chocolate sauce by melting chocolate and mixing with coconut butter.

6 Lightly break up the meringue to make pieces.

7 Assemble each serving by layering pieces of meringue, fresh berries and cream, drizzling a little chocolate sauce on top.

Chefs Note....
Cream of tartar is available in most larger supermarkets on the baking section.

Low Carb Doughnuts

CLEANSE DETOX & SHRED FAT

Ingredients

- 4oz/125g almond flour
- 2½oz/ 60g butter
- 2 eggs
- 2 tbsp sweetener (stevia or similar)
- ¼cup/60ml almond milk

- 1 tsp vanilla extract
- 1 tsp cinnamon
- 2 tsp baking powder
- Pinch of salt
- Oil for frying

Method

1 Preheat the oven to 180C/350F/Gas4.

2 Mix all the dry ingredients together.

3 Whisk the milk, eggs and butter, and slowly combine with powdered mixture until smooth.

4 Empty the mixture into a grease-lined doughnut tray. Bake for 15-20 minutes or until golden and remove to cool.

5 Before serving, deep-fry doughnuts for 20-30 seconds in oil until deeply golden.

6 Dust with a little extra cinnamon.

Chefs Note....
Deep-fry these just before serving, for a warm, delicious treat.

Coffee and Walnut Cake

CLEANSE DETOX & SHRED FAT

Ingredients

- 9 large eggs
- 1½oz/40g coconut flour
- 2 tbsp sweetener (stevia or similar)
- 1½oz/ 40g vanilla protein powder
- 2oz/50g butter

- ½oz/15g walnuts
- ½ tsp bicarbonate of soda
- ½ tsp cream of tartar
- ½ tsp vanilla extract
- 1 tsp espresso coffee powder

Method

1 Preheat oven to 165C/325F/Gas3.

2 Separate the yolk and egg whites into two different bowls.

3 Mix the egg whites with Cream of Tartar. Beat until stiff, shiny peaks begin to form.

4 In another bowl, mix yolks, vanilla extract, sweetener and coffee powder together.

5 Ground walnuts until medium-coarse in texture, and mix with flour and protein powder.

6 Slowly fold egg whites into flour mixture.

7 Melt and cool butter slightly, and begin to fold butter into cake mixture.

8 Bake for 30 minutes, or until golden, and allow to cool before serving.

Chefs Note....
Dust with powdered sweetener and coffee powder for an extra touch.

Blueberry Crumble

CLEANSE
DETOX &
SHRED FAT

Ingredients

- 1oz/25g almond meal
- 2 tsp butter
- 2 tbsp chopped walnuts

- ½ tsp baking powder
- 4oz/125g frozen blueberries
- 1 tsp sweetener (stevia or similar)

Method

1 Preheat oven to 150C/300F/Gas2.

2 Mix the almond meal, butter, sweetener, baking powder and chopped nuts until crumbs begin to form.

3 Place the blueberries in a large ramekin and top with crumble mixture.

4 Bake for 15-20 minutes, or until the topping Is golden brown, and blueberries start to bubble at the side.

Chefs Note....
Serve warm, with a scoop of ice cream.

Crème Brulee

SERVES 4

CLEANSE DETOX & SHRED FAT

Ingredients

- 2 cups/500ml double cream
- 2 tbsp sweetener (stevia or similar)
- 6 egg yolks
- Seeds from one vanilla pod
- 2 tsp powdered sweetener (stevia or similar)

Method

1 Preheat oven to 150C/300F/Gas2.

2 Beat eggs, sweetener and vanilla seeds until smooth and creamy in texture.

3 Heat double cream in a pan on a low heat, until almost boiling. Remove from heat and stir into egg mixture, beating until mixed.

4 Fill a large tray with hot water and place four ramekins on top – the water should not go beyond halfway up the ramekins.

5 Pour cream mixture into each ramekin. Bake for 30 minutes. Allow to cool and refrigerate (overnight if possible).

6 Before serving, sprinkle powdered sweetener on top. Place under a grill or use a blowtorch to caramelise the top. Serve immediately.

Chefs Note....
Serve with an optional scoop of sweetened whipped cream.

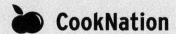 **CookNation**

Other CookNation titles

If you enjoyed
LOSE WEIGHT FOR GOOD: LOW CARB DIET FOR BEGINNERS
you may also enjoy other books from CookNation.

To browse the full catalogue visit
www.bellmackenzie.com

CONVERSION CHART: DRY INGREDIENTS

Metric	Imperial
7g	¼ oz
15g	½ oz
20g	¾ oz
25g	1 oz
40g	1½oz
50g	2oz
60g	2½oz
75g	3oz
100g	3½oz
125g	4oz
140g	4½oz
150g	5oz
165g	5½oz
175g	6oz
200g	7oz
225g	8oz
250g	9oz
275g	10oz
300g	11oz
350g	12oz
375g	13oz
400g	14oz

Metric	Imperial
425g	15oz
450g	1lb
500g	1lb 2oz
550g	1¼lb
600g	1lb 5oz
650g	1lb 7oz
675g	1½lb
700g	1lb 9oz
750g	1lb 11oz
800g	1¾lb
900g	2lb
1kg	2¼lb
1.1kg	2½lb
1.25kg	2¾lb
1.35kg	3lb
1.5kg	3lb 6oz
1.8kg	4lb
2kg	4½lb
2.25kg	5lb
2.5kg	5½lb
2.75kg	6lb

CONVERSION CHART: LIQUID MEASURES

Metric	Imperial	US
25ml	1fl oz	
60ml	2fl oz	¼ cup
75ml	2½ fl oz	
100ml	3½fl oz	
120ml	4fl oz	½ cup
150ml	5fl oz	
175ml	6fl oz	
200ml	7fl oz	
250ml	8½ fl oz	1 cup
300ml	10½ fl oz	
360ml	12½ fl oz	
400ml	14fl oz	
450ml	15½ fl oz	
600ml	1 pint	
750ml	1¼ pint	3 cups
1 litre	1½ pints	4 cups